A HOME-BAKED
CHRISTMAS

Delish

A HOME-BAKED
CHRISTMAS

56 DELICIOUS COOKIES,
CAKES & GIFTS FROM YOUR KITCHEN

CONTENTS

CHAPTER 1
CHRISTMAS
DESSERTS

PISTACHIO MERINGUE
WITH WHITE PEACHES AND BERRIES

PREP + COOK TIME 2 HOURS 15 MINUTES (+ COOLING) SERVES 10

2 cups heavy cream
4 medium white peaches, cut into
  thin wedges
4 ounces fresh blueberries
4 ounces fresh blackberries
2 tablespoons coarsely chopped
  pistachios, toasted

PISTACHIO MERINGUE
1 cup coarsely chopped pistachios
6 large egg whites
1½ cups superfine sugar
2 teaspoons corn starch
2 teaspoons vanilla extract
2 teaspoons white vinegar

1 Make pistachio meringue.
2 Beat cream in small bowl with
electric mixer until firm peaks
form. Place one meringue on
serving plate. Spread with half the
cream; top with half the peaches
and berries. Top with remaining
meringue, cream, fruit, and nuts.

PISTACHIO MERINGUE
Preheat oven to 250°F. Mark a
9-inch circle on two sheets of
parchment paper. Turn paper
over, place on two oven trays.
Process half the nuts until fine.
Beat egg whites in medium bowl
with electric mixer until soft peaks
form. Add sugar, a tablespoon at a
time, beating until sugar dissolves
between additions; beat until
mixture is thick and glossy. Beat in
corn starch, extract, and vinegar;
fold in ground nuts. Divide
meringue mixture between circles
on trays; spread evenly. Sprinkle
with remaining nuts. Bake
meringues about 1¼ hours. Cool
meringues in oven with door ajar.

TIP Make and assemble recipe at
least a day ahead; this will make
slicing it much easier.

FIG, ALMOND,
AND MASCARPONE TRIFLE

PREP + COOK TIME *1 HOUR 15 MINUTES (+ COOLING & REFRIGERATION)* **SERVES 6**

2 cups water
1 cup superfine sugar
2 whole star anise
12 medium fresh figs, halved
¼ cup almond-flavored liqueur
12 ladyfinger cookies

ALMOND PRALINE
½ cup slivered almonds, toasted
½ cup superfine sugar
2 tablespoons water

ZABAGLIONE CREAM
4 eggs, separated
½ cup superfine sugar
⅓ cup almond-flavored liqueur
1 pound mascarpone cheese

1 Combine the water, sugar, and star anise in large saucepan. Stir over heat until sugar is dissolved; bring to a boil. Add figs; simmer gently, uncovered, about 5 minutes or until tender. Cool; stir in liqueur. Remove figs from syrup; drain well. Reserve syrup. Place figs in large bowl.
2 Make almond praline.
3 Make zabaglione cream.
4 Dip one-third of the ladyfingers into fig syrup; place in single layer over 2-quart serving dish or in six 1-cup serving glasses. Top with one-third of zabaglione cream, one-third poached figs, and one-third almond praline. Repeat layering twice. Refrigerate at least 1 hour.

ALMOND PRALINE
Place nuts in single layer on greased oven tray. Combine sugar and the water in medium frying pan; stir over heat until sugar is dissolved. Bring to a boil; boil, uncovered, without stirring, until a deep golden color. Allow bubbles to subside, pour over nuts; cool. Break praline into pieces.

ZABAGLIONE CREAM
Beat egg yolks and sugar in medium heatproof bowl with electric mixer over medium saucepan of simmering water until pale. Add liqueur; beat until mixture has tripled in volume and holds ribbon shapes when beaters are lifted. Cool. Place mascarpone in large bowl; beat until smooth. Fold in egg yolk mixture. Beat egg whites in small bowl with electric mixer until soft peaks form; fold into mascarpone mixture, in two batches.

HONEY PANNA COTTA
WITH APRICOTS IN THYME SYRUP

PREP + COOK TIME *1 HOUR (+ COOLING & REFRIGERATION)* **SERVES** *8*

3 teaspoons powdered gelatin
¼ cup water
2⅓ cups buttermilk
½ cup heavy cream
½ cup honey

APRICOTS IN THYME SYRUP
2 cups water
½ cup honey
2 teaspoons fresh thyme leaves
12 small apricots, halved, pitted
1 tablespoon lemon juice

1 Sprinkle gelatin over the water in small heatproof cup; stand cup in small saucepan of simmering water, stir until gelatin dissolves.
2 Meanwhile, bring buttermilk and cream to a boil in medium saucepan; remove from heat. Whisk in honey and gelatin mixture; strain into large pitcher. Cool.

3 Divide buttermilk mixture between eight ⅔–cup glasses. Refrigerate about 6 hours or overnight until set.
4 Make apricots in thyme syrup.
5 Serve panna cotta topped with apricots and syrup.

APRICOTS IN THYME SYRUP
Bring the water, honey, and thyme to a boil in medium saucepan. Add apricots; simmer gently, uncovered, about 5 minutes or until almost tender. Remove from heat; add juice, cool. Refrigerate until cold.

CUSTARD FRUIT TARTS

PREP + COOK TIME *1 HOUR (+ REFRIGERATION & COOLING)* **MAKES** *24*

1¾ cups all-purpose flour
¼ cup confectioners' sugar
1½ sticks cold butter, chopped
   coarsely
1 egg yolk
2 teaspoons iced water,
   approximately
1 medium kiwi, peeled
2 ounces fresh raspberries
2 ounces fresh blueberries

CUSTARD CREAM
1 cup milk
1 teaspoon vanilla extract
3 egg yolks
⅓ cup superfine sugar
2 tablespoons pure corn starch
⅓ cup heavy cream, whipped
   to soft peaks

1 Process flour, sugar, and butter until crumbly. With motor operating, add egg yolk and enough of the water to make ingredients come together. Turn dough onto floured surface, knead gently until smooth. Wrap pastry in plastic; refrigerate 30 minutes.

2 Grease two 12-hole (1-tablespoon) mini muffin pans. Roll out half the pastry between sheets of parchment paper until ⅛-inch thick. Cut 2¼-inch rounds from pastry; press rounds into holes of one pan. Prick bases of shells well with a fork. Repeat with remaining pastry. Refrigerate 30 minutes.

3 Preheat oven to 425°F.

4 Bake shells about 12 minutes. Stand shells in pan 5 minutes before transferring to wire rack to cool.

5 Meanwhile, make custard cream.

6 Cut kiwi crosswise into eight slices; cut 1¼-inch rounds from slices. Divide custard cream into cases; top with fruit.

CUSTARD CREAM
Bring milk and vanilla extract to a boil in small saucepan. Meanwhile, beat egg yolks, sugar, and corn starch in small bowl with electric mixer until thick.

With motor operating, gradually beat in hot milk mixture. Return custard to pan; stir over heat until mixture boils and thickens. Cover surface of custard with plastic wrap, refrigerate 1 hour. Fold cream into custard, in two batches.

TIPS Pastry shells and custard cream can be made and stored separately, 2 days ahead; fold cream into custard just before using. Assemble tarts as close to serving time as possible—about an hour is good.

GLAZED FRUIT
STOLLEN

PREP + COOK TIME *1 HOUR 30 MINUTES (+ STANDING)* **MAKES** *2 LOAVES*
(EACH LOAF **MAKES** *12 SLICES)*

1¼ cups barely warm milk
½ ounce dried yeast
½ cup superfine sugar
4¾ cups bread flour
¼ teaspoon sea salt
2 sticks butter, softened slightly
2 eggs
¾ cup golden raisins
½ cup dried currants
½ cup finely chopped dried apricots
⅓ cup mixed candied citrus, diced
¼ cup red glacé cherries, quartered
⅓ cup slivered almonds, chopped
  coarsely
1 tablespoon finely grated lemon
  rind
8 ounces marzipan
1½ cups confectioners' sugar
2 tablespoons milk, extra

1 Combine milk, yeast, and 1
tablespoon of the sugar in small
bowl; cover, stand in a warm place
about 10 minutes or until mixture is
frothy.
2 Meanwhile, sift flour, salt, and
remaining sugar into large bowl;
rub in butter.
3 Stir yeast mixture and eggs into
flour mixture; mix to a soft, sticky
dough. Stir in fruit, nuts, and rind.
Place dough in oiled bowl, cover
with oiled plastic wrap; stand in
warm place about 1 hour or until
doubled in size.

4 Grease two baking sheets.
5 Turn dough onto floured surface,
knead about 5 minutes or until
smooth. Divide dough in half. Roll
each half into 8-inch x 12-inch
rectangle. Roll marzipan into two
10-inch logs; place along center of
dough. Fold dough over marzipan,
transfer to sheets. Cover with oiled
plastic wrap, stand in warm place
about 1 hour or until doubled in size.
6 Preheat oven to 400°F.
7 Bake stollen 15 minutes. Reduce
oven to 325°F. Bake an additional
25 minutes or until browned and
hollow sounding when tapped.
Stand on pans 5 minutes before
transferring to wire racks to cool.
8 Sift confectioners' sugar into
medium bowl; stir in extra milk.
Drizzle glaze over warm stollen.

TIPS Bread flour is a strong flour,
which means that it has a relatively
high gluten (protein) content. This
causes the bread to rise, giving it
shape and structure. It is available
from most supermarkets.
Stollen will keep in an airtight
container for up to a month. It's
delicious toasted lightly under the
broiler; serve buttered.

PANETTONE
WITH MASCARPONE AND RASPBERRIES

PREP TIME *30 MINUTES (+ REFRIGERATION)* **SERVES** *12*

1 panettone (about 2¼ pounds)
¼ cup orange-flavored liqueur
1½ pounds fresh raspberries
2 teaspoons confectioners' sugar

MASCARPONE FILLING
1½ pounds mascarpone cheese
¼ cup confectioners' sugar, sifted
3 egg whites

1 Make mascarpone filling.
2 Using a serrated knife, cut domed top off panettone; reserve for another use. Split remaining panettone crosswise into three layers.
3 Place base of panettone onto serving plate. Sprinkle with 1 tablespoon of liqueur; spread with one-third of filling and scatter with one-third of the raspberries. Top with another slice of panettone. Repeat to make another two layers, finishing with mascarpone filling. Refrigerate, loosely covered.
4 Remove panettone from refrigerator 30 minutes before serving. Top with remaining raspberries; dust with sifted confectioners' sugar.

MASCARPONE FILLING
Combine cheese and sifted sugar in large bowl. Beat egg whites in small bowl with electric mixer until soft peaks form. Fold egg whites into cheese mixture, in two batches.

TIPS We used Grand Marnier in this recipe but you could use any citrus-flavored liqueur you like.
This dessert is best made the day before or up to 5 hours before serving to allow the flavors to develop.
You can make it with all kinds of seasonal fruit such as mixed berries, sliced peaches, plums, nectarines, or mangos.
Store the unused panettone in plastic wrap and toast for breakfast.

WHITE CHRISTMAS
ICE CREAMS

PREP + COOK TIME *1 HOUR 15 MINUTES (+ COOLING & FREEZING)* **MAKES** *8*

1 vanilla bean
1¾ cups milk
2⅓ cups heavy cream
5½ ounces white chocolate,
    chopped
8 egg yolks
¾ cup superfine sugar
1 cup dried cranberries
2 tablespoons brandy
1 cup unsalted pistachios, shelled
2 teaspoons vegetable oil

1 Split vanilla bean lengthwise; scrape seeds into medium saucepan. Add pod, milk, cream, and 1½ ounces of the chocolate; bring to a boil, reduce heat to low.
2 Meanwhile, whisk egg yolks and sugar in medium bowl until thick and creamy; gradually whisk into hot milk mixture. Stir custard over low heat, without boiling, until thickened slightly. Cover surface of custard with plastic wrap; cool 20 minutes.

3 Strain custard into shallow container; discard pod. Cover with foil; freeze until almost firm.
4 Place custard in large bowl, chop coarsely; beat with electric mixer until smooth. Pour into deep container, cover; freeze until firm. Repeat process two more times.
5 Meanwhile, place cranberries and brandy in small bowl; stand 15 minutes.
6 Stir cranberry mixture and nuts into ice cream. Spoon ice cream into eight ¾-cup molds. Cover; freeze 3 hours or until firm.
7 Stir remaining chocolate and oil in small saucepan over low heat until mixture is smooth.
8 Dip each mold, one at a time, into a bowl of hot water for about 1 second. Turn ice creams onto serving plates; top with warm chocolate mixture.

CHEAT'S FROZEN
CHRISTMAS PUDDING

PREP TIME *30 MINUTES (+ FREEZING)* **SERVES 8**

1 quart vanilla ice cream, softened
1½ pounds fruit cake, crumbled
¼ cup brandy or rum

1 Line eight ¾-cup molds with plastic wrap, extending plastic about 1¼ inches over edge of molds.

2 Process ice cream, cake, and brandy until combined. Spoon ice cream mixture into molds. Cover with plastic wrap then foil; freeze overnight.

3 Turn puddings onto a parchment-paper-lined tray. Gently peel away plastic, transfer puddings to serving plates.

SERVING SUGGESTION
Serve with chocolate sauce or the choc-orange sauce on page 34.

FROZEN CHRISTMAS
PUDDING

PREP + COOK TIME *2 HOURS (+ COOLING, CHURNING, & FREEZING)* **SERVES 10**

1 vanilla bean
2½ cups heavy cream
1 cup milk
4 egg yolks
½ cup firmly packed light
brown sugar

CHOCOLATE ICE CREAM
1¼ cups heavy cream
¾ cup milk
2 teaspoons finely grated
orange rind
3 ounces finely chopped semi-
sweet chocolate
3 egg yolks
⅓ cup superfine sugar
¼ cup golden raisins
1 tablespoon rum or brandy
¼ cup quartered glacé cherries
¼ cup finely chopped mixed
candied citrus
1½ ounces finely chopped semi-
sweet chocolate, extra

1 Grease 2-quart metal pudding
basin or bowl. Line with plastic
wrap; place in freezer.
2 To make brown sugar ice cream,
split vanilla bean in half
lengthwise, scrape seeds into
medium saucepan. Add pod,
cream, and milk to pan; bring to a
boil; reduce heat to low.

3 Meanwhile, whisk egg yolks and
sugar in small bowl until pale;
gradually whisk into hot cream
mixture. Stir over low heat,
without boiling, about 10 minutes
or until mixture thickens and
coats the back of a spoon. Strain
custard into large heatproof bowl
set over large bowl of ice; discard
pod. Cover surface of custard with
plastic wrap; stand until cold.
4 Pour custard into ice cream
maker, churn according to
manufacturer's instructions (or
follow instructions in **TIPS**, see
next page). Spoon ice cream into
lined basin or bowl; freeze about 1
hour or until firm. Using a spatula,
press the ice cream into the sides
of the basin or bowl creating an
even layer that's hollow in the
center. Cover with foil, re-freeze.
5 Meanwhile, make chocolate
orange ice cream.
6 Fill brown sugar ice cream
cavity with chocolate orange ice
cream; smooth surface. Cover with
foil; freeze overnight.
7 Chill serving platter in freezer.
Turn basin onto platter; cover
with a hot, damp cloth. Gradually
pull plastic to ease pudding onto
platter; discard plastic.

CHOCOLATE ORANGE ICE CREAM

Bring cream, milk, and rind to a boil in medium saucepan. Remove from heat, add chocolate; stir until smooth. Meanwhile, whisk egg yolks and sugar in small bowl until pale; gradually whisk into hot cream mixture. Stir over low heat, without boiling, about 10 minutes or until mixture thickens and coats the back of a spoon. Strain custard into large heatproof bowl set over bowl of ice. Cover surface with plastic wrap; stand until cold. Pour custard into ice cream maker, churn according to manufacturer's instructions (or follow instructions in **TIPS**, see right). Spoon ice cream into large bowl, stir in raisins, rum, cherries, peel, and extra chocolate.

TIP If you don't have an ice cream maker, pour custard mixture into shallow pan, cover with foil, and freeze until almost set. Chop ice cream roughly and beat in large bowl with electric mixer, or process, until smooth. Return to pan and freeze again, repeating process once more. Freeze about 1 hour, then allow to soften slightly; spoon ice cream into pudding basin (or add additional ingredients) and follow the recipe.

(PHOTOGRAPH PAGE 25)

TIRAMISU
TORTE

PREP + COOK TIME *1 HOUR 10 MINUTES* (*+ COOLING & REFRIGERATION*) SERVES *12*

3 eggs
½ cup superfine sugar
¼ cup all-purpose flour
¼ cup self-rising flour
¼ cup corn starch
2 tablespoons instant coffee
  granules
¾ cup boiling water
⅓ cup marsala
2 tablespoons coffee-flavored
  liqueur
1 pound mascarpone cheese
⅓ cup confectioners' sugar
1¼ cups heavy cream

1 Preheat oven to 350°F. Grease deep 9-inch square cake pan with butter.
2 Beat eggs in small bowl with electric mixer about 10 minutes or until thick and creamy; gradually add sugar, one tablespoon at a time, beating until sugar dissolves between additions. Transfer to large bowl.
3 Sift flours twice. Sift flours over egg mixture; fold ingredients together. Spread mixture into pan.
4 Bake sponge about 25 minutes. Turn sponge immediately onto parchment-covered wire rack, turn top-side up to cool.

5 Meanwhile, dissolve coffee in the water in small heatproof bowl. Stir in marsala and liqueur; cool.
6 Beat mascarpone and confectioners' sugar in small bowl with electric mixer until smooth. Beat in cream and ⅓ cup of the coffee mixture.
7 Split sponge in half vertically, then split each sponge in half horizontally. Place one of the cake rectangles on serving plate, cut-side up; brush with a quarter of the remaining coffee mixture, then spread with ⅔ cup of mascarpone mixture. Repeat layering process finishing with the cake, cut-side down, and remaining mascarpone mixture spread on top and sides of cake. Refrigerate cake 2 hours.
8 Decorate cake with coarsely chopped candied or toffee almonds, if you like.

TIP Alternate the sponge pieces when layering so that the cut side of the sponge is on different sides on each layer; this will ensure the torte is even and does not lean to one side.

LEMON AND RASPBERRY
SEMIFREDDO

PREP + COOK TIME *1 HOUR 15 MINUTES (+ FREEZING)* **SERVES 12**

2 tablespoons finely grated
  lemon rind
½ cup lemon juice
1 cup superfine sugar
8 egg yolks
¼ cup limoncello liqueur
2⅓ cups heavy cream
1 cup frozen raspberries,
  crumbled coarsely
2 ounces fresh raspberries
fresh mint sprigs

CANDIED LEMON SLICES
1 medium lemon, sliced thinly
¼ cup superfine sugar
¾ cup water

1 Grease 3½-inch x 10-inch loaf
pan. Line with parchment paper,
extending paper 2 inches over
edges of pan.
2 Stir rind, juice, and sugar in
small saucepan until sugar is
dissolved; bring to a boil. Remove
from heat, cool 10 minutes. Strain
lemon syrup into small pitcher;
discard solids.
3 Beat egg yolks in small bowl
with electric mixer until light and
fluffy. Beat in lemon syrup and
liqueur; transfer to large bowl.
4 Beat cream in medium bowl
with electric mixer until soft peaks
form. Fold cream into lemon
mixture, cover bowl with foil;
freeze about 4 hours or until thick.

5 Stir frozen raspberries into
cream mixture; pour into loaf pan.
Cover with plastic wrap, then foil;
freeze overnight or until firm.
6 Meanwhile, make candied
lemon slices.
7 Stand semifreddo at room
temperature 5 minutes before
turning out. Top with candied
lemon, fresh raspberries, and
mint.

CANDIED LEMON SLICES
Place lemon in small saucepan,
cover with cold water. Bring to a
boil; simmer, uncovered, 1 minute,
drain. Combine sugar and the
water in small saucepan; stir over
low heat until sugar dissolves.
Add lemon slices, bring to a boil;
remove from heat. Stand 30
minutes or until slices are
translucent; drain. Place lemon
slices on wire rack over tray; cool.
Store, covered with parchment
paper, at room temperature.

TIP Limoncello liqueur is an Italian
lemon-flavored liqueur made from
the peel only of fragrant lemons.
The peels are steeped in a good-
quality clear alcohol then diluted
with sugar and water. It's available
from good liquor outlets and Italian
food stores.

FRUIT CAKE
ICE CREAM TERRINE

PREP TIME *15 MINUTES (+ FREEZING)* **SERVES 6**

1-pound loaf fruit cake, cut into
¾-inch-thick slices
2 tablespoons orange-flavored
liqueur
2 quarts vanilla ice cream,
softened
1 tablespoon finely grated
orange rind

1 Line 5½-inch x 8½-inch loaf pan
with plastic wrap.
2 Brush cake slices with liqueur.
3 Place ice cream in large bowl;
stir in rind.
4 Spread half the ice cream
mixture into pan; top with cake
slices, then remaining ice cream.
Cover with plastic wrap; freeze
until firm. Using hot knife, cut
terrine into six slices.

TIP Serve with fresh mixed
berries.

CHOC-ORANGE SAUCE

PREP + COOK TIME *15 MINUTES*
MAKES *2 CUPS*

12½ ounces semi-sweet chocolate, chopped coarsely
2 tablespoons butter, chopped coarsely
1 teaspoon vanilla extract
1 cup heavy cream
2 tablespoons orange-flavored liqueur

1 Stir chocolate and butter until smooth in medium heatproof bowl over medium saucepan of simmering water.
2 Stir in extract, cream, and liqueur. Serve warm.

SPICED RUM BUTTER

PREP TIME *10 MINUTES*
MAKES *2½ CUPS*

2 sticks unsalted butter, softened
½ cup firmly packed light brown sugar
2 teaspoons each ground cinnamon and ground ginger
½ teaspoon each ground nutmeg and ground cloves
2 tablespoons dark rum

1 Beat butter in small bowl with electric mixer until as white as possible.
2 Beat in sugar, spices, and rum until light and fluffy.

(OPPOSITE, TOP, CHOC-ORANGE SAUCE; BOTTOM, SPICED RUM BUTTER)

VANILLA BEAN CUSTARD

PREP + COOK TIME *25 MINUTES*
MAKES *2½ CUPS*

1 vanilla bean
1¼ cups heavy cream
¾ cup milk
6 egg yolks
½ cup superfine sugar

1 Split vanilla bean in half lengthwise; scrape seeds into medium saucepan, add pod, cream, and milk. Bring to a boil, then strain mixture into large pitcher. Discard pod.
2 Meanwhile, whisk egg yolks and sugar in medium heatproof bowl. Gradually whisk hot milk mixture into egg mixture.
3 Return custard mixture to pan; stir over low heat until mixture is thick enough to coat the back of a spoon. Serve warm or cold.

HAZELNUT HARD SAUCE

PREP TIME *10 MINUTES*
MAKES *1¾ CUPS*

1 stick unsalted butter, softened
1 cup confectioners' sugar, sifted
2 tablespoons heavy cream
2 tablespoons hazelnut-flavored liqueur

1 Beat butter and sifted sugar in small bowl with electric mixer until as white as possible.
2 Beat in cream and liqueur.

(OPPOSITE, TOP, VANILLA BEAN CUSTARD; BOTTOM, HAZELNUT HARD SAUCE)

CHAPTER 2

CHRISTMAS CAKES

HAZELNUT MUD CAKE
WITH FUDGE FROSTING

PREP + COOK TIME *2 HOURS (+ COOLING)* SERVES *12*

11½ ounces semi-sweet chocolate, chopped coarsely
1¾ sticks butter, chopped coarsely
¾ cup firmly packed light brown sugar
¾ cup water
¾ cup all-purpose flour
¼ cup self-rising flour
½ cup ground hazelnuts
2 eggs
⅓ cup hazelnut-flavored liqueur

FUDGE FROSTING
3 tablespoons butter, chopped coarsely
1 tablespoon water
⅓ cup firmly packed light brown sugar
2 tablespoons hazelnut-flavored liqueur
1 cup confectioners' sugar
2 tablespoons cocoa powder

1 Preheat oven to 300°F. Grease deep 8-inch round cake pan; line base and side with parchment paper.
2 Stir chocolate, butter, sugar, and the water in medium saucepan over low heat until smooth. Cool 15 minutes.
3 Stir sifted flours, ground hazelnuts, eggs, and liqueur into chocolate mixture. Pour into pan.
4 Bake about 1 hour 35 minutes. Stand cake in pan 5 minutes; turn, top-side up, onto wire rack to cool.
5 Meanwhile, make fudge frosting.
6 Spread cake with frosting.

FUDGE FROSTING
Stir butter, the water, and brown sugar in small saucepan over heat until sugar dissolves. Remove from heat; stir in liqueur. Sift icing sugar and cocoa into small bowl; gradually stir in hot butter mixture until smooth. Cover; refrigerate about 15 minutes or until frosting thickens. Beat frosting with a wooden spoon until spreadable.

TIP We used Frangelico for this recipe, but you can use any hazelnut or chocolate-flavored liqueur you like.

GRAND MARNIER
FRUIT CAKE

PREP + COOK TIME 5 HOURS 40 MINUTES (+ STANDING & COOLING)

3 cups golden raisins
1½ cups candied citrus peel, diced
¾ cup coarsely chopped dark raisins
¾ cup coarsely chopped pitted dried dates
⅔ cup coarsely chopped pitted prunes
½ cup coarsely chopped glacé apricots
⅔ cup coarsely chopped glacé pineapple
½ cup slivered almonds
½ cup coarsely chopped walnuts
1 tablespoon finely grated orange rind
½ cup superfine sugar
¼ cup orange juice
½ cup Grand Marnier
2 sticks butter, softened
½ cup firmly packed light brown sugar
5 eggs
2 cups all-purpose flour
2 tablespoons Grand Marnier, extra
2 pounds ready-made white fondant
1 egg white, beaten lightly
½ cup confectioners' sugar, sifted
10-inch round covered cake board
decorative ribbon
silver drageés

1 Combine fruit, nuts, and rind in large bowl.
2 Cook sugar in large frying pan over low heat, without stirring, until it begins to melt, then stir until sugar is melted and browned lightly. Remove from heat, slowly stir in juice; return to low heat, stir until sugar dissolves (do not boil). Stir in liqueur.
3 Pour syrup over fruit mixture. Cover with plastic wrap; store mixture in a cool, dark place for 10 days, stirring every day.
4 Preheat oven to 300°F. Line base and sides of deep 9-inch round or deep 8-inch square cake pan with two layers of parchment paper, extending paper 2 inches above edge of pan.

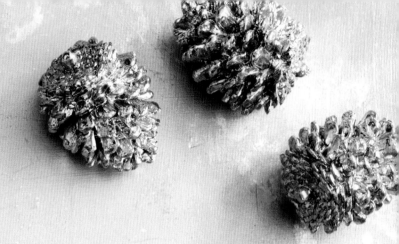

5 Beat butter and brown sugar in small bowl with electric mixer until just combined; beat in eggs, one at a time. Stir butter mixture into fruit mixture. Mix in sifted flour; spread mixture into pan. Tap pan firmly on counter to settle mixture into pan; level cake mixture with wet spatula.

6 Bake cake about 3½ hours. Remove cake from oven, brush with extra liqueur; cover hot cake with foil, then turn upside down to cool overnight.

7 Trim top of cake with sharp knife to ensure it sits flat when turned upside down. Mix a little fondant and cold water to a sticky paste. Spread about 2 tablespoons of this mixture into the center of a sheet of parchment paper about 2 inches larger than the cake; position cake upside down on paper.

8 Using spatula and small pieces of fondant, patch any holes on cake.

9 Brush egg white evenly over cake. Knead white fondant on surface dusted with confectioners' sugar until smooth; roll to ¼-inch thickness. Lift icing onto cake with rolling pin, smoothing icing over cake with hands dusted with confectioners' sugar. Using sharp knife, cut excess icing away from base of cake.

10 Mix scraps of fondant and cold water to a sticky paste. Spread about 2 tablespoons of paste in center of board; center cake on prepared board. Move the cake to the correct position on the board; using sharp craft knife or scalpel, carefully cut away excess parchment paper extending around base of cake.

11 Secure ribbon around cake using pins (remove before cutting cake). Push drageés gently into icing in the design of your choice.

(PHOTOGRAPH PAGES 42 & 43)

TWAS the night

before Christmas . . . and you forgot the fruit cake.

Head straight to the kitchen with this recipe: it doesn't require

weeks of soaking dried fruit and it's out of the oven in 45 minutes—perfect.

Cut it up on Christmas Day and no one will know the difference.

NIGHT BEFORE
FRUIT CAKE

PREP + COOK TIME *1 HOUR 15 MINUTES (+ COOLING)* **MAKES** *24*

3 cups diced mixed dried and glacé fruit, soaked briefly in hot water

⅓ cup finely chopped candied ginger

10 tablespoons butter, chopped coarsely

⅔ cup firmly packed light brown sugar

1 teaspoon finely grated lemon rind

2 tablespoons lemon juice

½ cup brandy

½ teaspoon baking soda

3 eggs, beaten lightly

½ cup mashed banana

1½ cups all-purpose flour

½ cup self-rising flour

½ cup slivered almonds

1 Combine dried and glacé fruit, ginger, butter, sugar, rind, juice, and ⅓ cup of the brandy in medium saucepan; stir over heat until butter is melted and sugar dissolved. Bring to a boil, remove from heat; stir in soda. Transfer to large bowl; cool.

2 Preheat oven to 325°F. Grease 8-inch x 12-inch rectangular pan; line base and two long sides with parchment paper, extending paper 2 inches above sides.

3 Stir egg and banana into fruit mixture, then stir in sifted flours. Spread mixture into pan; sprinkle with nuts.

4 Bake cake about 45 minutes. Brush hot cake with remaining brandy, cover with foil; cool in pan. Cut cake into 24 squares. Dust with sifted confectioners' sugar to serve, if you like.

TIP You need 1 large overripe banana to get the amount of mashed banana required for this recipe.

RICH CHOCOLATE
FRUIT CAKE

PREP + COOK TIME *3 HOURS 50 MINUTES (+ STANDING & REFRIGERATION)* **SERVES** *20*

1¾ pounds canned pitted black
  cherries in syrup
1 cup dark raisins, chopped
  coarsely
¾ cup finely chopped pitted
  dried dates
½ cup golden raisins
½ cup finely chopped pitted
  prunes
1 cup dried figs, chopped finely
1 cup marsala
1 cup pecans
1½ sticks butter, softened
2 teaspoons finely grated orange
  rind
1¼ cups firmly packed dark
  brown sugar
3 eggs, at room temperature
1¼ cups all-purpose flour
½ cup self-rising flour
2 tablespoons cocoa powder
2 teaspoons pie spice
3 ounces semi-sweet chocolate,
  chopped finely

GANACHE
7 ounces semi-sweet chocolate,
  chopped coarsely
½ cup heavy cream

1 Drain cherries; reserve ⅓ cup
syrup. Quarter cherries. Combine
cherries with remaining fruit,
¾ cup of the marsala, and
reserved cherry syrup in large
bowl. Cover; stand overnight.

2 Preheat oven to 300°F. Grease
deep 9-inch round cake pan; line
with two layers of parchment
paper, extending paper 2 inches
over edge of pan.
3 Process half the nuts until
ground finely; chop the remaining
nuts coarsely.
4 Beat butter, rind, and sugar in
small bowl with electric mixer
until combined; beat in eggs, one
at a time. Mix butter mixture into
fruit mixture; stir in sifted dry
ingredients, chocolate, and ground
and chopped nuts. Spread mixture
into pan.
5 Bake cake about 3 hours. Brush
hot cake with remaining marsala,
cover with foil; cool in pan.
6 Make ganache.
7 Spread cake with ganache; top
with chocolate decoration (see
tips below). Dust with sifted
confectioners' sugar to serve, if
you like.

GANACHE
Stir ingredients in small saucepan
over low heat until smooth.
Refrigerate, stirring occasionally,
about 20 minutes or until
spreadable.

TIPS Store un-iced cake in the refrigerator for up to 3 months. Once iced, the cake can be stored in the fridge for 2 weeks. Cut and bring to room temperature before serving. We painted a branch of real holly roughly with melted dark chocolate to make the inedible decoration on the cake. Remove cake from fridge, then top with the chocolate decoration. Do not eat the holly!

IRISH PUDDING
CAKE

PREP + COOK TIME *4 HOURS (+ STANDING & COOLING)* SERVES *8*

1½ cups pitted dried dates,
  chopped coarsely
1½ cups dark raisins,
  chopped coarsely
1¼ cups pitted prunes,
  chopped coarsely
1 cup dried currants
¾ cup golden raisins
1 large apple, grated coarsely
1½ cups Irish whiskey
1¼ cups firmly packed light
  brown sugar
1½ sticks butter, softened
3 eggs, beaten lightly
½ cup ground hazelnuts
1½ cups all-purpose flour
1 teaspoon ground nutmeg
½ teaspoon baking soda
½ teaspoon each ground ginger
  and ground cloves

1 Combine fruit and 1 cup of the whiskey in large bowl. Cover with plastic wrap; stand overnight.
2 Preheat oven to 250°F. Grease deep 8-inch round cake pan; line with two layers of parchment paper, extending paper 2 inches over edge of pan.
3 Stir remaining whiskey and ½ cup of the sugar in small saucepan over heat until sugar dissolves; bring to a boil. Cool syrup 20 minutes.

4 Meanwhile, beat butter and remaining sugar in small bowl with electric mixer until just combined (do not overbeat). Beat in eggs, a little at a time. Add butter mixture to fruit mixture; stir in ground hazelnuts, sifted dry ingredients, and ½ cup of the cooled syrup. Spread mixture into pan.
5 Bake cake about 3½ hours. Brush cake with reheated remaining syrup, cover cake with foil; cool in pan.

TIP If your dilemma is whether to make a Christmas cake or pudding, this recipe is the best of both worlds because it's just as delicious served hot as a pudding or cold as a cake. And it's not necessary to make it ages in advance: starting to prepare it a day or so ahead is just fine. It will keep, covered, in the refrigerator for several months. Although the inclusion of Irish whiskey makes it authentic, Scotch, dark rum, or brandy are fine substitutes.

FRUIT CAKE
(THREE-IN-ONE FRUIT MIX)

PREP + COOK TIME *3 HOURS* (+ *COOLING*) SERVES *20*

4¼ cups three-in-one fruit mix
1½ sticks butter, melted
3 eggs, beaten lightly
1½ cups all-purpose flour
½ teaspoon baking soda
¼ cup brandy

1 Preheat oven to 280°F. Line base and side of deep 8-inch round cake pan with two layers of parchment paper, extending paper 2 inches over edge of pan.
2 Place fruit mix in large bowl. Stir in butter, eggs, and sifted flour and soda. Spread mixture into pan; level top.
3 Bake cake about 2½ hours. Brush hot cake with brandy. While still hot, cover cake, still in its pan, tightly with foil, then wrap in a towel and cool overnight.

THREE-IN-ONE-FRUIT MIX
2⅓ cups golden raisins
2 cups dried currants
2⅓ cups coarsely chopped dark raisins
1 cup finely chopped dried dates
¾ cup finely chopped pitted prunes
1 cup finely chopped dried figs
2 large apples, grated coarsely
¼ cup golden syrup or molasses
2¼ cups firmly packed dark brown sugar
2 cups brandy
2 teaspoons ground ginger
1 teaspoon each ground nutmeg and ground cinnamon

Combine ingredients in large bowl; cover tightly with plastic wrap. Store in a cool, dark place for a month (or longer, if desired) before using. Stir mixture every two or three days.

TIPS Turn cake out of pan, remove lining paper from side of cake. Wrap tightly in plastic wrap. Place cake in an airtight container to protect it. Store in the refrigerator for up to 3 months, or freeze for up to a year. Thaw frozen cake in the refrigerator for 2 days.

WHITE CHRISTMAS
SLICE

PREP TIME *20 MINUTES (+ REFRIGERATION)* **MAKES 32**

1 pound white chocolate,
  chopped coarsely
1 cup crisped rice cereal
1 cup golden raisins
1 cup desiccated coconut
⅔ cup finely chopped dried
  apricots
½ cup halved red glacé cherries

1 Grease 8-inch x 12-inch
rectangular pan; line base and
long sides with parchment
paper, extending paper 2 inches
above sides.

2 Melt chocolate in large
heatproof bowl set over large
saucepan of simmering water.
Remove from heat; quickly stir in
remaining ingredients.
3 Press mixture firmly into pan.
Refrigerate 2 hours or until firm.

GLUTEN-FREE FRUIT AND ALMOND LOAVES

PREP + COOK TIME *2 HOURS 35 MINUTES* (*+ STANDING & COOLING*) MAKES *2*

2 pounds mixed dried fruit
1 tablespoon finely grated
   orange rind
⅔ cup sweet sherry
9 tablespoons butter, softened
⅔ cup firmly packed dark
   brown sugar
4 eggs, at room temperature
3 ounces marzipan, chopped
   coarsely
1 small apple, grated coarsely
¾ cup ground almonds
1¼ cups gluten-free all-purpose
   flour
1 cup blanched whole almonds
¼ cup sweet sherry, extra

1 Combine fruit, rind, and sherry
in large bowl; mix well.
Cover with plastic wrap; stand in
cool, dark place for one week,
stirring every day.

2 Preheat oven to 300°F. Line
bases and sides of two 3¼-inch x
8½-inch loaf pans with two layers
of parchment paper, extending
paper 2 inches above sides.
3 Beat butter and sugar in small
bowl with electric mixer until just
combined. Beat in eggs, one at a
time. Mix butter mixture into fruit
mixture. Stir in marzipan, apple,
ground almonds, and sifted flour.
Spread mixture into pans;
decorate with nuts.
4 Bake loaves about 2 hours.
Brush hot loaves with extra
sherry, cover with foil; cool in
pans.

GOLDEN GLACÉ
FRUIT CAKE

PREP + COOK TIME *4 HOURS (+ COOLING)* SERVES *20*

5 ounces glacé pear, chopped finely

5 ounces red and green glacé cherries, chopped finely

5 ounces glacé peach, chopped finely

4 ounces glacé ginger, chopped finely

4 ounces glacé figs, chopped finely

⅔ cup brandy or orange-flavored liqueur

8 ounces unsalted butter, softened

1 cup superfine sugar

4 eggs, at room temperature

1⅔ cups all-purpose flour

1 cup ground almonds

1 Preheat oven to 300°F. Line base and side of deep 8-inch round cake pan with two layers of parchment paper, extending paper 2 inches over edge of pan.

2 Combine fruit and ½ cup of the brandy in large bowl.

3 Beat butter and sugar in small bowl with electric mixer until combined. Beat in eggs one at a time. Add butter mixture to fruit mixture; mix well. Stir in sifted flour and ground almonds, in two batches. Spread mixture into pan; smooth top.

4 Bake cake about 3 hours. Brush hot cake with remaining brandy. While still hot, cover cake, still in its pan, tightly with foil; cool in pan.

TIP Cake will keep in an airtight container for up to a month. Cake can be frozen for 3 months.

CHOCOLATE DRAMBUIE
FRUIT CAKE

PREP + COOK TIME *4 HOURS 50 MINUTES (+ STANDING & COOLING)* **SERVES 36**

2⅓ cups golden raisins

2¼ cups dark raisins, chopped coarsely

1⅔ cups dried currants

1½ cups pitted prunes, chopped coarsely

1½ cups pitted dried dates, chopped coarsely

¾ cup candied citrus peel, diced

⅔ cup red glacé cherries, quartered

1⅓ cups Drambuie

⅓ cup honey

1 tablespoon finely grated lemon rind

2 sticks butter, softened

1½ cups firmly packed dark brown sugar

6 eggs, at room temperature

3 ounces semi-sweet chocolate, grated coarsely

1¼ cups pecans, chopped coarsely

2 cups all-purpose flour

1 cup self-rising flour

¼ cup cocoa powder

1 cup pecan halves

6 glacé cherries

1 Combine fruit, 1 cup of the liqueur, honey, and rind in large bowl. Cover with plastic wrap; stand in cool, dark place for one week, stirring every day.

2 Preheat oven to 250°F. Grease six-hole ¾-cup jumbo muffin pan.

Grease deep 9-inch round or deep 8-inch square cake pan; line base and side(s) with four layers of parchment paper, extending paper 2 inches above side(s).

3 Beat butter and sugar in medium bowl with electric mixer until just combined. Beat in eggs, one at a time. Mix butter mixture into fruit mixture with chocolate and nuts. Stir in sifted dry ingredients, in two batches.

4 Fill each muffin pan hole, level to the top, with mixture; spread remaining mixture into cake pan. Decorate tops with pecans and glacé cherries.

5 Bake muffins 1½ hours (cake can stand while muffins are baking). Brush hot muffins with some of the remaining liqueur, cover with foil; cool in pan.

6 Increase oven to 300°F; bake large cake 3 hours. Brush hot cake with remaining liqueur, cover with foil; cool in pan.

TIPS If you don't want to make the muffins, spread all the cake mixture into a deep 10-inch round or deep 9-inch square cake pan, and bake about 4 to 4½ hours. Cake can be made up to 3 months ahead; store in an airtight container in therefrigerator, or freeze for up to a year.

CELEBRATION
CHRISTMAS CAKES

PREP + COOK TIME 3 HOURS 15 MINUTES (+ STANDING & COOLING) MAKES 2

3 cups golden raisins
1¾ cups dark raisins
1¾ cups pitted dried dates
1 cup dried currants
¼ cup candied orange
⅔ cup red glacé cherries
¼ cup glacé ginger
¼ cup dried apricots
½ cup orange-flavored liqueur
2 sticks butter, softened
1 cup firmly packed light brown sugar
5 large eggs
1½ cups all-purpose flour
⅓ cup self-rising flour
1 teaspoon pie spice
2 tablespoons orange-flavored liqueur, extra
2 pounds ready-made white fondant
1 large egg white
½ cup confectioners' sugar
8-inch square cake board
silver drageés
silver ribbon

1 Chop all fruit the same size as a raisin. Combine fruit and liqueur in large bowl; cover with plastic wrap, stand overnight.
2 Preheat oven to 300°F. Line two deep 6-inch square cake pans with three layers of parchment paper, extending paper 2 inches above sides of pans.
3 Beat butter and brown sugar in small bowl with electric mixer until combined; beat in eggs, one at a time. Mix butter mixture into fruit mixture. Stir in sifted flours and spice; divide mixture between pans.
4 Bake cakes about 2 hours. Brush hot cakes with extra liqueur, cover with foil, turn upside down on counter; cool in pan.
5 Trim top of one cake if necessary to make it flat. Mix a walnut-sized piece of white fondant with enough cold water to make a sticky paste. Spread half of this mixture into the center of a sheet of parchment paper about 2 inches larger than the cake; position cake top-side down on paper. Using spatula and small pieces of white fondant, patch any holes in the cake.
6 Brush egg white evenly over cake. Knead half the remaining white fondant on surface dusted with sifted confectioners' sugar until smooth; roll to ¼-inch thickness. Lift icing onto cake with rolling pin, smoothing icing over cake with hands dusted with confectioners' sugar. Cut excess fondant away from base of cake.
7 Mix fondant scraps with cold water to make a sticky paste. Spread half the paste in center of cake board; center cake on board. Cut away excess parchment paper around base of cake.

8 Gently push a 2½-inch bell-shaped cutter three-quarters of the way into icing. Using a small sharp knife, carefully remove about half the icing inside the bell shape. Carefully pull cutter out of icing. Push dragées gently into icing to fill bell. Secure half the ribbon around cake using pins. Repeat with second cake.

CHOCOLATE AND SHERRY
CHERRY CAKE

PREP + COOK TIME 1 HOUR 50 MINUTES (+ STANDING & COOLING)
MAKES 2 (EACH CAKE SERVES 6)

9½ ounces fresh cherries, pitted, quartered
½ cup sweet sherry
6 tablespoons butter, chopped coarsely
6½ ounces semi-sweet chocolate, chopped coarsely
1⅓ cups firmly packed light brown sugar
4 large eggs
⅔ cup self-rising flour
½ cup cocoa powder
⅔ cup sour cream

CHOCOLATE GANACHE
6½ ounces semi-sweet chocolate, chopped coarsely
½ cup heavy cream
1 tablespoon corn syrup

1 Combine cherries and sherry in small bowl; cover, stand at room temperature 3 hours or overnight.
2 Preheat oven to 325°F. Grease two deep 6-inch square cake pans; line bases and sides with parchment paper, extending paper 2 inches over sides.

3 Melt butter and chocolate in medium heatproof bowl over medium saucepan of simmering water. Remove from heat; stir in sugar. Using electric mixer, beat in eggs, one at a time. Add sifted dry ingredients; beat on low speed until combined. Beat in sour cream, then stir in cherry mixture. Pour mixture evenly into pans.
4 Bake cakes about 1 hour 20 minutes; cool cakes in pans.
5 Make chocolate ganache.
6 Place cakes on serving plates; spread ganache over cakes.

CHOCOLATE GANACHE
Stir ingredients in small heatproof bowl over small pan of simmering water until smooth. Stand about 20 minutes or until spreadable.

TIPS Corn syrup helps give the ganache a glossy look. It is available in the baking aisle of most supermarkets.
Cakes may be stored in an airtight container in the refrigerator for up to a month, or frozen for up to 3 months. The ganache will not be as glossy after freezing.

GLUTEN- AND DAIRY-FREE
SPICY FRUIT CAKE

PREP + COOK TIME *3 HOURS (+ STANDING & COOLING)* **SERVES** *20*

1¼ cups golden raisins
1 cup finely chopped pitted
 dried dates
1 cup dark raisins, chopped
 coarsely
¾ cup dried currants
1 cup coarsely chopped glacé
 apricots
1 cup tokay or other dessert
 wine
6 ounces dairy-free margarine
1 cup firmly packed dark
 brown sugar
3 eggs
1 cup ground almonds
1½ cups rice flour
1 teaspoon cream of tartar
½ teaspoon baking soda
1 teaspoon ground nutmeg
½ teaspoon each ground ginger
 and ground cloves

1 Combine fruit and ¾ cup of the tokay in large bowl, cover with plastic wrap; stand overnight.
2 Preheat oven to 250°F. Line deep 9-inch round cake pan with two layers of parchment paper, extending paper 2 inches above side.
3 Beat margarine and sugar in small bowl with electric mixer until combined; beat in eggs, one at a time. Mix butter mixture into fruit mixture; mix in ground almonds and sifted dry ingredients. Spread mixture into pan.
4 Bake cake about 2½ hours. Brush hot cake with remaining tokay, cover with foil; cool in pan. Serve dusted with sifted confectioners' sugar, if you like.

TIPS Tokay is a sweet white fortified wine.
Store cake in the refrigerator for up to 3 months. Cut the cake straight from the fridge, then bring to room temperature before serving.

YULE LOG

4½ ounces semi-sweet chocolate, melted
½ cup all-purpose flour
3 teaspoons each ground ginger and pie spice
¼ teaspoon ground cloves
3 eggs
⅔ cup superfine sugar
¼ cup hazelnut-flavored liqueur
1 tablespoon confectioners' sugar

HAZELNUT FILLING
8 ounces mascarpone cheese
8 ounces cream cheese, softened
¼ cup cocoa powder, sifted
½ cup chocolate hazelnut spread
¼ cup hazelnut-flavored liqueur

TUILE LEAVES
2 tablespoons butter, softened
¼ cup superfine sugar
1 egg white, beaten lightly
⅓ cup all-purpose flour

1 Preheat oven to 425°F. Grease two 10-inch x 12-inch jelly-roll pans; line bases with parchment paper, extending paper 2 inches over long sides.
2 Spread chocolate in a thin layer in one of the pans. Refrigerate about 7 minutes or until chocolate is firm but slightly pliable. Tear chocolate into small pieces; refrigerate until needed.
3 Meanwhile, sift flour and spices into small bowl. Beat eggs and ½ cup of the sugar in small bowl with electric mixer about 5 minutes or until thick and creamy. Transfer to large bowl; si flour mixture over egg mixture, then fold into the egg mixture. Pour into pan; bake about 15 minutes. Reduce oven to 350°F.
4 Place large sheet of parchmer paper on wire rack; sprinkle paper with remaining sugar. Turn cake onto baking paper, remove lining paper, immediately roll up cake from short side; cool.
5 Meanwhile, make hazelnut filling; reserve 1½ cups. Make tuile leaves.
6 Unroll cake, brush with liqueur; spread with remaining filling, leaving a 1¼-inch borde on one short side. Roll up from opposite short side, using pape as a guide. Transfer to serving platter. Spread reserved filling over cake. Decorate with chocolate pieces. Using a skew make spiral patterns on each e of log. Refrigerate 1 hour. Dus log with sifted confectioners' sugar just before serving. Decorate log with tuile leaves.

HAZELNUT FILLING
Beat ingredients in small bowl with electric mixer until thick and creamy.

TUILE LEAVES

Using a leaf-shaped cutter as a template, trace around cutter on thick cardboard. Cut out the center of the shape, leaving a stencil. Line oven tray with parchment paper. Stir butter and sugar in medium bowl; stir in egg white. Stir in sifted flour until smooth. Drop 1 teaspoon of mixture into leaf cutout on tray. Spread mixture thinly to make leaf. Carefully lift template from leaf, position on tray about 1¼ inches away from the first leaf. (Make and bake three leaves at a time.) Bake in 350°F oven about 8 minutes or until browned lightly. Working quickly, slide a spatula under tuile to loosen, then place over a rolling pin to form curved shapes. Cool on rolling pin 5 minutes before transferring to wire rack to cool. Repeat with remaining mixture.

CHAPTER 3
CHRISTMAS
COOKIES &
EDIBLE GIFTS

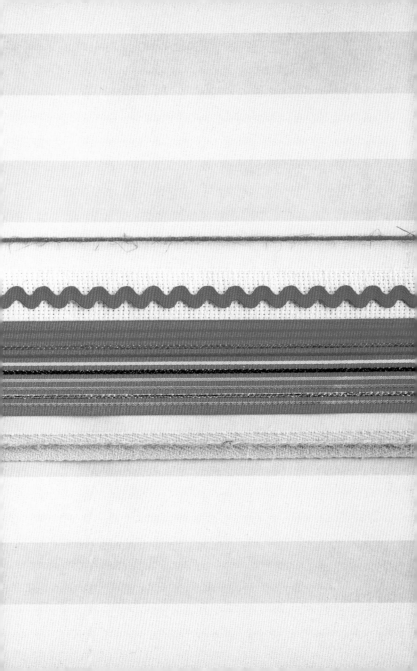

GINGERBREAD
HOUSE
·················

PREP + COOK TIME *3 HOURS 30 MINUTES (+ REFRIGERATION & STANDING)*
MAKES 1 HOUSE (SERVES 20)

paper, for house template
2¼ cups self-rising flour
1½ teaspoons ground ginger
1 teaspoon ground cinnamon
¾ teaspoon ground cloves
½ teaspoon ground nutmeg
6 tablespoons butter, chopped
coarsely
½ cup firmly packed dark brown
sugar
¼ cup molasses
1 large egg, beaten lightly
4 large bamboo skewers
1¼ cups milk chocolate melts,
melted
½ cup superfine sugar
2 tablespoons water
cooking-oil spray
2 tablespoons coarsely chopped
dried cranberries
1 tablespoon coarsely chopped
pistachios
1¼ cups white chocolate melts,
melted
14-inch round or square cake
board
3 cups whole pecans
1½ cups desiccated coconut
2 teaspoons confectioners' sugar

1 Cut paper templates for gingerbread house: two 5¼-inch x 7-inch rectangles for the roof, two 4-inch x 6¼-inch rectangles for the side walls, and two 4-inch x 7¼-inch rectangles for the front and back walls. Trim front and back walls to make two 4-inch high gables. Cut two 1½-inch windows from each side wall. Cut door out of one side wall, reserving door cut-out piece. Cut out a 1½-inch square for window sills.

2 Process flour, spices, and butter until crumbly. Add brown sugar, molasses, and egg; process until combined. Turn dough onto floured surface; knead until smooth. Cover with plastic wrap; refrigerate 1 hour.

3 Preheat oven to 350°F.

4 Roll dough, in several batches, between sheets of parchment paper until ¼-inch thick. Peel away top paper and use templates to cut shapes from dough. Remove excess dough. Slide parchment paper with shapes onto oven trays.

5 Bake about 12 minutes or until shapes are barely firm (they become crisp when cool).

6 While shapes are still warm and soft, use the tip of a sharp knife to trim shapes to straighten sides. Cut square into four even lengths to form window sills. Transfer shapes to wire racks to cool.

7 Secure two crossed skewers to back of each roof piece with some of the milk chocolate. Allow to set.

8 Stir superfine sugar and the water in small saucepan over low heat until sugar is dissolved. Bring to a boil; boil, uncovered, until toffee turns golden brown. Remove from heat.

9 To make wreath, line an oven tray with parchment paper. Position a 2½-inch round metal cutter on one side of tray. Place a smaller ¾-inch round metal cutter in center of larger cutter; spray with oil. Pour a little toffee between cutters to form a ring. Drizzle a ¾-inch x 4-inch long strip of toffee over tray. Sprinkle ring and strip of toffee with cranberries and pistachios; drizzle with a little more toffee if necessary. Pour remaining toffee over tray; cool.

10 Push center out of wreath, discard. Break large piece of toffee into four large squares. Secure toffee to inside of windows with some of the milk chocolate.

11 Assemble house on board, securing roof and walls together with milk chocolate. Secure door to house with milk chocolate. Spread a little white chocolate over the back of pecans; layer, in rows, over roof. Secure wreath to side of house with a little milk chocolate. Secure window sills to window edges with white chocolate. Break toffee strip into pieces, secure to window sills with a little white chocolate. Decorate board around house with coconut to resemble snow. Dust house with sifted confectioners' sugar.

TIP Gingerbread can be made up to a week ahead; store in an airtight container. The house can be assembled 5 days ahead; keep covered in a cool dry place. In hot humid weather, the toffee should be made on the day of serving.

(PHOTOGRAPH PAGE 73)

CINNAMON AND SOUR CHERRY
MACAROONS

PREP + COOK TIME *1 HOUR 15 MINUTES (+ REFRIGERATION, STANDING & COOLING)*
MAKES 20

3 egg whites
¼ cup superfine sugar
1¼ cups confectioners' sugar
1 cup ground almonds
½ teaspoon ground cinnamon

SOUR CHERRY CURD

½ cup drained pitted morello
  sour cherries
3 large egg yolks
⅓ cup superfine sugar
1 tablespoon lemon juice
2 teaspoons kirsch
2 ounces unsalted butter,
  chopped coarsely

CINNAMON SUGAR

2 tablespoons confectioners' sugar
½ teaspoon ground cinnamon

1 Make sour cherry curd and cinnamon sugar.
2 Grease oven trays; line with parchment paper.
3 Beat egg whites in small bowl with electric mixer until soft peaks form. Add superfine sugar, beat until sugar is dissolved. Transfer mixture to large bowl. Fold in sifted confectioners' sugar, ground almonds, and cinnamon, in two batches.
4 Spoon mixture into piping bag fitted with ¾-inch plain tube. Pipe 1½-inch rounds about ¾-inch apart on trays. Tap trays on counter so macaroons spread slightly. Dust macaroons with half the sifted cinnamon sugar; stand about 30 minutes or until dry to touch.
5 Meanwhile, preheat oven to 300°F.
6 Bake macaroons about 20 minutes; cool on trays.
7 Sandwich macaroons with sour cherry curd; dust with remaining sifted cinnamon sugar.

SOUR CHERRY CURD

Blend or process cherries until smooth; you will need 2 tablespoons puree for this recipe. Place egg yolks and sugar in medium heatproof bowl over medium saucepan of simmering water; whisk until thick and sugar is dissolved. Whisk in cherry puree, juice, and kirsch. Add butter; whisk about 5 minutes or until mixture is thick and holds the trail of the whisk. Refrigerate until firm.

CINNAMON SUGAR

Combine ingredients in small bowl.

TIP Unfilled macaroons will keep in an airtight container for about a week. Filled macaroons will keep in an airtight container in the refrigerator for up to 2 days.

BROWNIE
BOMBS

PREP + COOK TIME *1 HOUR (+ COOLING & REFRIGERATION)* **MAKES 50**

Preheat oven to 350°F. Grease deep 8-inch square cake pan; line base and sides with parchment paper. Stir 1 stick chopped butter and 6½ ounces chopped semi-sweet chocolate in medium saucepan over low heat until smooth; transfer to large bowl, cool 10 minutes. Stir in ⅔ cup superfine sugar, 2 lightly beaten large eggs, and 1¼ cups sifted all-purpose flour. Spread mixture into pan; bake about 30 minutes. Cool in pan. Cut brownie into large pieces; process with ⅓ cup dark rum until mixture comes together. Roll heaped teaspoons of mixture into balls. Freeze for 10 minutes. Melt 6½ ounces chopped semi-sweet chocolate; dip balls into chocolate to coat. Refrigerate until set. Drizzle with 2 ounces melted white chocolate, decorate with pieces of glacé cherry.

CHRISTMAS
COOKIES

PREP + COOK TIME *30 MINUTES (+ REFRIGERATION)* **MAKES 28**

Grease oven trays; line with parchment paper. Beat 2 sticks softened butter, ¾ cup superfine sugar, and 1 large egg in small bowl with electric mixer until light and fluffy; transfer to large bowl. Stir in 2¼ cups sifted all-purpose flour. Knead dough on floured surface until smooth. Cover; refrigerate 30 minutes. Preheat oven to 350°F. Roll heaped teaspoons of mixture into 6-inch log shapes. Twist two pieces of dough together, shape into canes and wreaths. Place on trays. Bake about 12 minutes; cool on trays. Sprinkle hot cookies with 2 tablespoons cinnamon sugar.

(OPPOSITE, TOP, BROWNIE BOMBS; BOTTOM, CHRISTMAS COOKIES)

CHRISTMAS
MUFFINS

**PREP + COOK TIME *40 MINUTES*
MAKES *12***

Preheat oven to 400°F. Grease
12-hole (⅓-cup) muffin pan. Sift
2½ cups self-rising flour into
medium bowl; rub in 6 tablespoons
chopped butter. Gently stir in 1
cup superfine sugar, 1¼ cups
buttermilk, and 1 beaten large egg.
Gently stir in 1 cup mixed coarsely
chopped glacé fruit. Spoon mixture
into pan holes; bake about 20
minutes. Stand muffins 5 minutes
before turning, top-side up, onto
wire rack to cool. Roll 8 ounces
ready-made white fondant out to
¼-inch thick; cut out 1¾-inch stars.
Brush tops of muffins with 2
tablespoons warmed, strained
apricot jam; top with icing stars.
Dust with sifted confectioners'
sugar, if you like.

FRUIT NUT
CLUSTERS

**PREP + COOK TIME *30 MINUTES (+
REFRIGERATION)* MAKES *36***

Line three 12-hole mini muffin
pans with liners. Stir 9
tablespoons chopped butter,
½ cup superfine sugar, and
2 tablespoons honey in small
saucepan over low heat until sugar
dissolves. Combine 3½ cups
cornflakes, ½ cup coarsely
chopped dried cranberries, ½ cup
toasted sliced almonds, ½ cup
coarsely chopped toasted
pistachios, and ⅓ cup finely
chopped glacé peach in large bowl.
Stir in butter mixture. Spoon
mixture into paper cases;
refrigerate until set.

(OPPOSITE, TOP, CHRISTMAS MUFFINS;
BOTTOM, FRUIT NUT CLUSTERS)

MACADAMIA AND PECAN
SHORTBREAD

PREP + COOK TIME *45 MINUTES* **MAKES** *24*

2 sticks butter, softened
½ cup superfine sugar
2 teaspoons vanilla extract
2 cups all-purpose flour
½ cup rice flour
⅓ cup finely chopped macadamias
½ cup finely chopped pecans
2 tablespoons superfine sugar,
  extra

1 Preheat oven to 325°F. Lightly grease two oven trays.
2 Beat butter, sugar, and extract in small bowl with electric mixer until pale and fluffy. Transfer mixture to large bowl; stir in sifted flours and nuts, in two batches. Press mixture together. Turn dough onto lightly floured surface; knead gently until smooth.

3 Divide dough in half. Roll each portion between sheets of parchment paper into 9-inch rounds; place on trays. Mark each round into 12 wedges, prick with a fork. Using floured fingers, pinch a frill around each shortbread, sprinkle with extra sugar.
4 Bake shortbread about 20 minutes. Stand on trays 10 minutes before transferring to wire racks to cool.

TIPS Use a cake pan or plate to mark, then cut the dough into a neat round.
Shortbread will keep in an airtight container for up to a month.

CHRISTMAS COOKIES

PREP + COOK TIME *50 MINUTES (+ REFRIGERATION)* **MAKES** *32*

1 vanilla bean
2 sticks butter, softened
¾ cup superfine sugar
1 large egg
1 tablespoon water
2¼ cups all-purpose flour
3 ounces individually wrapped
  sugar-free fruit drops, assorted
  colors

1 Split vanilla bean lengthwise; scrape seeds into medium bowl with butter, sugar, egg, and the water. Beat with electric mixer until combined. Stir in sifted flour, in two batches. Knead dough on floured surface until smooth. Cover with plastic wrap; refrigerate 30 minutes.

2 Preheat oven to 350°F. Line two oven trays with parchment paper.

3 Using a rolling pin, gently tap the wrapped candies to crush them slightly. Unwrap candies, separate by color into small bowls.

4 Roll dough between sheets of parchment paper to ¼-inch thickness. Cut shapes from dough using 3¼-inch long Christmas tree cutter; place cookies on oven trays. Using a 1½-inch long Christmas tree or ¾-inch star cutter, cut out the center of each tree to make windows. Use a skewer to make a small hole in top of each tree for threading through ribbon, if you like.

5 Bake trees 7 minutes. Remove trays from oven; fill each window with a few of the same-colored candies. Bake an additional 5 minutes or until browned lightly. Cool trees on trays.

SEA SALT AND
CASHEW CARAMELS

PREP + COOK TIME *30 MINUTES (+ COOLING)* **MAKES** *40*

1½ cups superfine sugar
1½ cups heavy cream
¼ cup corn syrup
1½ cups unsalted roasted cashews
2 teaspoons sea salt

1 Grease a 7¼-inch x 11¼-inch jelly-roll pan. Line base and sides with parchment paper, extending paper 2 inches over sides.
2 Stir sugar, cream, and corn syrup in medium saucepan until sugar is dissolved. Bring to a boil; boil, uncovered, until mixture reaches 248°F on a candy thermometer.
3 Add nuts and half the salt, do not stir. Pour caramel into lined pan; sprinkle with remaining salt. Cool.
4 Use a warm oiled sharp knife to cut caramel into pieces.

TIPS Corn syrup is available in the baking aisle of most supermarkets. Store caramels between layers of wax paper in an airtight container in a cool dry place for up to a week.
When packaging as a gift, layer between sheets of wax paper or parchment paper.

ANGEL GIFT TAG
COOKIES

PREP + COOK TIME *50 MINUTES (+ REFRIGERATION & STANDING)* **MAKES 20**

1 stick butter, softened
¾ cup superfine sugar
1 large egg
1¾ cups all-purpose flour
⅓ cup self-rising flour
2 tablespoons sugar
red ribbon

LEMON ROYAL ICING
2 cups confectioners' sugar
1 egg white
2 teaspoons lemon juice

1 Beat butter, superfine sugar, and egg in small bowl with electric mixer until light and fluffy. Stir in sifted flours, in two batches. Knead dough on floured surface until smooth. Cover with plastic wrap; refrigerate 30 minutes.
2 Preheat oven to 350°F. Line two oven trays with parchment paper.
3 Roll dough between sheets of parchment paper to ¼-inch thickness. Cut 3¼-inch x 4½-inch angel shapes from dough; cut two ¾-inch moon shapes across center of angel shapes for threading ribbon. Place on oven trays.

4 Bake cookies about 12 minutes. Cool on trays.
5 Meanwhile, make lemon royal icing.
6 Spread angel cookies with icing; sprinkle with sugar crystals. Stand at room temperature until icing is set; thread ribbon through holes.

LEMON ROYAL ICING
Sift confectioners' sugar through fine sieve onto sheet of parchment paper. Beat egg white in small bowl with electric mixer until foamy; beat in sugar, a tablespoon at a time. Stir in juice.

TIP Store cookies in an airtight container for up to 2 days to keep them crisp until you want to attach them to your gifts.

CHOC-ORANGE
TRUFFLES
WITH DRUNKEN PRUNES AND GINGER

PREP + COOK TIME *1 HOUR (+ STANDING & REFRIGERATION)* **MAKES** *24*

½ cup heavy cream
14½ ounces semi-sweet chocolate, chopped coarsely
½ cup cocoa powder

BOOZY PRUNES AND GINGER
⅓ cup finely chopped pitted prunes
2 tablespoons finely chopped glacé ginger
2 teaspoons finely grated orange rind
1 tablespoon orange-flavored liqueur

1 Make boozy prunes and ginger.
2 Combine cream and chocolate in medium heatproof bowl. Place bowl over medium saucepan of simmering water; stir until mixture is smooth. Stand at room temperature until mixture starts to thicken. Stir in prune mixture. Refrigerate about 2 hours or until firm.
3 Sift cocoa into medium bowl. Roll level tablespoons of chocolate mixture into balls; roll in cocoa. Place on tray; refrigerate until firm.

4 Remove from refrigerator 30 minutes before serving. Dust with a little extra sifted cocoa.

BOOZY PRUNES AND GINGER
Combine ingredients in small bowl; cover, stand overnight.

TIPS Grand Marnier or Cointreau can be used for the orange-flavored liqueur.
Store truffles in an airtight container in the refrigerator for up to 3 weeks. Truffles, without cocoa coating, can be frozen for up to 3 months. Remove from freezer 1 hour before serving.

CHOCOLATE
FIG PANFORTE

PREP + COOK TIME *1 HOUR 10 MINUTES (+ STANDING)* **SERVES 20**

¾ cup all-purpose flour
2 tablespoons cocoa powder
2 teaspoons ground cinnamon
1¾ cups coarsely chopped
  dried figs
¼ cup finely chopped glacé orange
1 cup blanched almonds, toasted
1 cup hazelnuts, toasted
1 cup pecans, toasted
⅓ cup honey
⅓ cup superfine sugar
⅓ cup firmly packed light brown
  sugar
2 tablespoons water
3 ounces semi-sweet chocolate,
  melted

1 Preheat oven to 300°F. Grease deep 8-inch round cake pan; line base with parchment paper.

2 Sift flour, cocoa, and cinnamon into large bowl; stir in fruit and nuts. Combine honey, sugars, and the water in small saucepan; stir over low heat until sugar dissolves. Simmer, uncovered, without stirring, 5 minutes. Pour hot syrup then chocolate into nut mixture; mix well.

3 Press mixture firmly into pan; press an 8-inch round of parchment paper on top.

4 Bake 40 minutes; cool in pan. Remove panforte from pan, discard parchment paper; wrap in foil. Stand overnight before cutting into thin wedges to serve.

JEWELED
MACAROONS

PREP + COOK TIME *45 MINUTES (+ COOLING)* **MAKES** *24*

1 egg white
¼ cup superfine sugar
¾ cup shredded coconut
2 tablespoons each finely chopped
  glacé apricot, glacé pineapple,
  glacé red cherries, and glacé
  green cherries
2 tablespoons finely chopped
  toasted, unsalted pistachios

1 Preheat oven to 300°F. Line two
12-hole (1-tablespoon) mini muffin
pans with paper cases.
2 Beat egg white in small bowl
with electric mixer until soft peaks
form; gradually add sugar, beating
until sugar dissolves. Fold coconut
and half the combined fruit and
nuts into egg white mixture.

3 Divide mixture between paper
cases. Sprinkle with remaining
fruit and nut mixture.
4 Bake about 20 minutes; cool
macaroons in pans.

TIPS Cover macaroons with foil
halfway through baking time if
fruit on top starts to brown.
You need about 1½ ounces of each
glacé fruit.

CHRISTMAS CAKES

PREP + COOK TIME *3 HOURS 20 MINUTES (+ STANDING & COOLING)* **MAKES** *8*

2⅓ cups golden raisins
2⅓ cups coarsely chopped dark
  raisins
1½ cups dried currants
1½ cups pitted prunes, chopped
  coarsely
⅓ cup mixed candied citrus peel
½ cup red glacé cherries,
  quartered
2 cups tokay or port
2 cups firmly packed dark brown
  sugar
2 sticks butter, softened
6 large eggs
¾ cup pecans, chopped coarsely
2 cups all-purpose flour
¾ cup self-rising flour
½ cup cocoa powder
8 ounces ready-made white
  fondant

1 Combine fruit, 1½ cups of the
tokay, and ½ cup of the brown
sugar in large bowl. Cover; stand
overnight or for several days.
2 Preheat oven to 300°F. Line
bases and sides of eight deep
4-inch square cake pans with two
layers of parchment paper,
extending paper ¾ inch over sides.
3 Beat butter and remaining sugar
in large bowl with electric mixer
until combined. Beat in eggs, one at
a time. Stir butter mixture into fruit
mixture. Stir in nuts and sifted dry

ingredients, in two batches. Divide
mixture into pans; smooth tops.
4 Bake cakes about 1¾ hours.
Brush hot cakes with remaining
tokay. Cover cakes, in pans, tightly
with foil; turn cakes upside down
to cool overnight.
5 To decorate, roll fondant between
sheets of parchment paper to ⅛-inch
thick; cut ½-inch thick ribbons,
attach to cake tops with a little
water. Using 1¼-inch star cutters,
cut stars from fondant. Brush back
of stars with a little water; attach to
top of ribbons. Stand for several
hours or until dry. Wrap sides of
cakes with a Christmas ribbon.

TO STORE UN-ICED CAKES
Turn cakes out of pan, remove
lining paper from side of cakes.
Wrap tightly in plastic wrap. Place
cakes in an airtight container to
protect them. Store in the
refrigerator for up to 3 months, or
freeze for up to a year. Thaw frozen
cakes in the refrigerator for 2 days.

TIPS Tokay is a sweet white
fortified wine.
This recipe will also make one deep
8-inch square or one deep 9-inch
round cake. Line pan with two
layers of parchment paper. Bake
about 3 hours.

SPICED WREATH
COOKIES

PREP + COOK TIME *1 HOUR (+ REFRIGERATION)* **MAKES 40**

1 stick butter, softened
½ cup firmly packed light brown
   sugar
½ cup molasses
1 large egg, separated
2 cups all-purpose flour
½ cup self-rising flour
1 teaspoon baking soda
2 teaspoons ground ginger
1 teaspoon ground cinnamon
¼ teaspoon ground cardamom
2 tablespoons raw sugar
⅓ cup sliced almonds

1 Preheat oven to 350°F. Line oven trays with parchment paper.
2 Beat butter, brown sugar, molasses, and egg yolk in small bowl with electric mixer until pale and creamy. Transfer to large bowl. Stir in sifted flours, baking soda, and spices. Turn dough onto floured surface, knead until smooth. Cover with plastic wrap, refrigerate 30 minutes.

3 Divide dough into two portions; roll each portion separately on lightly floured surface until ⅛-inch thick. Cut out rounds using 3-inch fluted cutter. Use 1¼-inch fluted cutter to cut an inner circle from each disc. Transfer to trays. Brush tops of dough with lightly beaten egg white; sprinkle half the cookies with raw sugar and remaining cookies with nuts. Bake about 10 minutes or until browned lightly. Stand 5 minutes, then transfer to wire racks to cool.

TIP Store cookies in an airtight container for up to 2 weeks.

MINCE PIES
(THREE-IN-ONE FRUIT MIX)

PREP + COOK TIME *1 HOUR (+ REFRIGERATION & STANDING)* **MAKES** *12*

1 cup all-purpose flour
1 tablespoon confectioners' sugar
1 tablespoon custard powder or
   instant vanilla pudding mix
6 tablespoons cold butter,
   chopped coarsely
1 large egg, separated
1 tablespoon iced water,
   approximately
1 cup three-in-one fruit mix (page
   53)
1 teaspoon finely grated lemon
   rind
1 tablespoon white (granulated)
   sugar

1 Grease 12-hole (2 tablespoon) jumbo muffin tin.
2 Process flour, confectioners' sugar, custard powder, and butter until crumbly. Add egg yolk and enough of the water to make ingredients come together. Knead dough on lightly floured surface until smooth. Cover with plastic wrap; refrigerate 30 minutes.
3 Preheat oven to 400°F.

4 Roll two-thirds of pastry between sheets of parchment paper until ⅛-inch thick. Cut 3-inch rounds from pastry. Re-roll pastry scraps if necessary to make 12 rounds. Press rounds into the bases of the muffin tin, reserve pastry scraps.
5 Combine fruit mix and rind in medium bowl. Drop level tablespoons of mixture into pastry cases.
6 Roll reserved pastry until ⅛-inch thick. Cut out 1¾-inch stars with a cutter. Place stars on pies; brush with egg white, sprinkle with white sugar.
7 Bake pies about 20 minutes or until browned lightly. Stand pies in pan 5 minutes before transferring to wire rack to cool.

TIP Store pies in an airtight container for a week, or freeze for up to 3 months; thaw pies overnight in the refrigerator.

PASSIONFRUIT CREAM
COOKIES

PREP + COOK TIME *45 MINUTES (+ REFRIGERATION & COOLING)* **MAKES 25**

1 stick butter, softened
2 teaspoons finely grated lemon
   rind
⅓ cup superfine sugar
2 tablespoons golden syrup or
   molasses
1 cup self-rising flour
⅔ cup all-purpose flour
¼ cup passionfruit pulp

PASSIONFRUIT CREAM
2 tablespoons passionfruit pulp
6 tablespoons butter, softened
1 cup confectioners' sugar

1 Beat butter, rind, and sugar in small bowl with electric mixer until light and fluffy. Add golden syrup, beat until combined. Stir in sifted dry ingredients and passionfruit pulp.
2 Turn dough onto floured surface, knead gently until smooth. Divide dough in half; roll each portion between sheets of parchment paper to ¼-inch thickness. Refrigerate 30 minutes.
3 Preheat oven to 350°F. Grease oven trays; line with parchment paper.

4 Cut 1½-inch fluted rounds from each portion of dough; place about 1 inch apart on trays.
5 Bake cokies about 10 minutes. Cool on trays.
6 Meanwhile, make passionfruit cream.
7 Spoon passionfruit cream into piping bag fitted with ¼-inch fluted tube. Pipe cream onto half the cookies; top with remaining cookies. Serve dusted with a little extra sifted confectioners' sugar, if you like.

PASSIONFRUIT CREAM
Strain passionfruit pulp through fine sieve into small bowl, discard seeds. Beat butter and sugar in small bowl with electric mixer until light and fluffy. Beat in passionfruit juice.

TIP You need about six passionfruits for this recipe.

CHAPTER 4
CHRISTMAS
DECORATIONS

ON THE
FIRST DAY
OF CHRISTMAS

❄ ⋯⋯   ⋯⋯ ❄

SILVER SPRAYED TWIGS
or tree branches make a great modern Christmas tree.
YOU WILL NEED a handful of tree branches
from the garden, roadside, or from a flower shop,
a can of silver spray paint from a craft store, newspaper,
SILVER AND GLASS DECORATIONS, scissors,
white or silver ribbon, and a vase. PLACE THE TWIGS or branches
on a large sheet of newspaper in a well-ventilated room.
Spray paint the twigs until well covered, then leave to dry for 1 hour.
TURN THE BRANCHES over and spray the underside so all surfaces
are silver. Leave to dry for an additional 30 minutes.
This can be repeated if necessary to ENSURE FULL COVERAGE.
ARRANGE THE TWIGS in a vase (choose a neutral color such as
white or clear glass), and turn the twigs until you have a "tree"
shape you are happy with. CUT THE RIBBON
of your choice into lengths (you will need as many lengths of ribbons
as there are DECORATIONS).
Loop a strip of ribbon through each ornament
and tie the ends together, HANG THE ORNAMENTS all over
the tree, carefully sliding the ribbons over
different twigs.

O CHRISTMAS TREE
O CHRISTMAS TREE

NOT EVERYONE HAS
room for a large tree so why not buy
a small tree and use it as a TABLE SETTING.
YOU WILL NEED a small Christmas tree
(available from lots and many supermarkets),
a large flower pot, garden urn, or ornate bucket,
and a small bag of pebbles (available from garden centers),
as well as SCISSORS AND ORNAMENTS.
PLACE THE STEM of the tree in the flower pot or bucket and
fill the space around with pebbles OR SMALL STONES
to keep the tree in an upright position.
Using scissors, trim the tips from any branches that stick out
irregularly to give the tree that CLASSIC TREE SHAPE.
HANG A SELECTION of small ornaments at intervals on the tree.
Choose a SIMPLE COLOR PALETTE of
two contrasting colors such as the
GOLD AND GREEN pictured here.

CHRISTMAS WRAPPING

SPRUCE UP CHRISTMAS PRESENTS
WITH A SPLASH OF CHRISTMAS FOLIAGE.
Using foliage as a pretty decoration on
your presents adds a personal touch that your
friends and family will really appreciate.

YOU WILL NEED your gifts, wrapping paper,
scissors, adhesive tape, pruning shears,
a basket or bag, and green ribbon.

WRAP ALL YOUR PRESENTS WITH THE
SAME OR SIMILAR WRAPPING PAPER.
Using the shears, snip a few leaves from garden
bushes or roadside trees.

PICK THOSE WITH VIBRANT GREEN FOLIAGE
and keep an eye out for any with
red berries or flowers for a truly festive feel.

TRIM EACH SPRIG to fit within the size
of the present,
place in the center of the present,
and tie in place.

THE
STOCKINGS
WERE HUNG
BY THE CHIMNEY
WITH CARE

CHILDREN LOOK FORWARD
to Christmas morning
to discover all the treats in their stocking.
Selecting stocking fillers is a
universal **JOY OF PARENTS** at Christmas.
If you don't have a fireplace, get creative and
HANG THE STOCKINGS
from a coat rack or hall tree. You will need
Christmas stockings **FOR EVERY CHILD**
and a variety of small presents.
LOOP THE STOCKING around the hooks
on a stand or coat hook to secure them and
fill with individually wrapped
SMALL GIFTS.

DECK THE HALLS WITH BOUGHS OF HOLLY

A HALLWAY CAN BE TRANSFORMED
by hanging some beautiful ornaments
from an existing CHANDELIER OR LAMP SHADE.
YOU WILL NEED a minimum of 10 ornaments of your choice,
a selection of colored ribbon, scissors, and masking tape.
FOR A CHANDELIER—cut the ribbon
into lengths and thread each ornament
with ribbon (each ribbon can be a different length)
leaving the ends untied.
Using a stepladder to safely REACH THE CHANDELIER,
carefully loop the ribbon around each arm
of the chandelier and tie into a knot allowing each
ornament to HANG FREELY.
FOR A LAMP SHADE—cut ribbon into lengths
and tie one end to each ornament.
Using a stepladder to safely reach the lamp shade,
attach the other END OF THE RIBBON
to the inside of the lamp shade.
ATTACH with masking tape, pressing down
well to SECURE IN PLACE.

THE FIRST NOEL
❄ ···· THE ANGELS DID SAY ···· ❄

MAKE YOUR OWN winter wonderland table decoration.
For this you will need a bell jar or a GLASS CAKE STAND
with a dome lid, a plate or base a little larger than
the dome, SOME FAKE SNOW (available online, search for fake snow)
and some SMALL CHRISTMAS DECORATIONS
such as a wooden house, fir trees, animals, or small figurines
(available from Christmas shops).
MAKE UP A SMALL AMOUNT of fake snow by following
packet instructions. Arrange a "hill" scene.
PLACE THE DOME on top to complete your winter wonderland
DECORATION.

❄ ·········· JOY ·········· ❄
TO THE WORLD

RED AND WHITE CANDIES look really festive arranged in
different jars on a fireplace mantel or WINDOW SILL.
YOU WILL NEED a selection of red and white candies
from your local candy store, a selection of clean JAM JARS
or medicine jars with lids, and tongs. Wash the
jam jars or MEDICINE JARS to remove any labels
and dry well. Arrange the candies in
LAYERS OR COLORS in the jars and
top with lids. Place a pair of tongs
NEARBY.

SILENT NIGHT
❄ ·········· HOLY NIGHT ·········· ❄

CREATE FALLING SNOWFLAKES with
assorted white doilies.
YOU WILL NEED at least 12 lace or fabric doilies,
a bottle of fabric stiffener
to harden the doilies (available from craft stores),
a small foam roller and tray (from the hardware store), newspaper,
parchment paper, scissors, and WHITE OR SILVER RIBBON.
Lay the newspaper on a flat surface
and top with two long sheets
of parchment paper to cover the length of the surface.
LAY THE DOILIES in the middle of the
parchment paper, leaving a gap between each one.
Place some stiffener in the tray and, using the roller,
coat a doily thoroughly.
Flip over and repeat on the other side.
Leave to dry overnight or until totally dry and hardened.
Cut 12 different lengths of white or silver ribbon
and tie one end to the doily, threading it through a hole in the lace trim.
Attach masking tape to the other end of the ribbon;
hang half of the doilies at the top of
the window frame and attach the remaining
doilies to the curtain rod.
This will give you two rows of falling SNOWFLAKES.

JINGLE BELLS
❄ ·········· JINGLE BELLS ·········· ❄

ADD A SPLASH OF COLOR
to your hallway with a bell jar
filled with colorful Christmas ornaments.
For this you will need a bell jar or GLASS CAKE STAND
with a dome lid, lots of
CHRISTMAS ORNAMENTS of any color, a plate
a little larger than the dome
(unless using a cake stand), and a helping hand.
One person will need to hold THE BELL JAR or dome
upside down while it is filled as full as
possible with ORNAMENTS.
GIVE THE JAR A GOOD SHAKE
to close up any gaps.
Place a plate over the open end and carefully turn
the JAR OR DOME the right way
up to create a colorful domed DECORATION.

INDEX

CONVERSION CHART

MEASURES

All cup and spoon measurements are level. The most accurate way to measure dry ingredients is to use a spoon to fill the measuring cup, without packing or scooping with the cup, and leveling off the top with a straight edge.

When measuring liquids, use a clear glass or plastic liquid measuring cup with markings on the side.

INGREDIENTS

Unless otherwise indicated in the recipe, always work with room temperature ingredients. Cold liquids added to butter can cause any batters and icings to break.

We use large eggs averaging 2 ounces each. Do not substitute extra large, as the higher amount of protein and volume of the whites can make baked goods tough.

DRY MEASURES

METRIC	IMPERIAL
15g	½oz
30g	1oz
60g	2oz
90g	3oz
125g	4oz (¼lb)
155g	5oz
185g	6oz
220g	7oz
250g	8oz (½lb)
280g	9oz
315g	10oz
345g	11oz
375g	12oz (¾lb)
410g	13oz
440g	14oz
470g	15oz
500g	16oz (1lb)
750g	24oz (1½lb)
1kg	32oz (2lb)

LIQUID MEASURES

METRIC	IMPERIAL
30ml	1 fluid oz
60ml	2 fluid oz
100ml	3 fluid oz
125ml	4 fluid oz
150ml	5 fluid oz (¼ pint/1 gill)
190ml	6 fluid oz
250ml	8 fluid oz
300ml	10 fluid oz (½ pint)
500ml	16 fluid oz
600ml	20 fluid oz (1 pint)
1000ml (1 liter)	1¾ pints

LENGTH MEASURES

3mm	⅛in
6mm	¼in
1cm	½in
2cm	¾in
2.5cm	1in
5cm	2in
6cm	2½in
8cm	3in
10cm	4in
13cm	5in
15cm	6in
18cm	7in
20cm	8in
23cm	9in
25cm	10in
28cm	11in
30cm	12in (1ft)

OVEN TEMPERATURES

These oven temperatures are only a guide for conventional ovens. For fan-forced ovens, check the manufacturer's manual.

	°F (FAHRENHEIT)	°C (CELSIUS)
Very slow	250	120
Slow	275–300	150
Moderately slow	325	160
Moderate	350–375	180
Moderately hot	400	200
Hot	425–450	220
Very hot	475	240

HEARST BOOKS
New York

An Imprint of Sterling Publishing
387 Park Avenue South
New York, NY 10016

DELISH

Elizabeth Shepard   Executive Director

Content contained in this book was originally published by ACP Magazines Limited
and is reproduced with permission.

Photography by Ian Wallace

U.S. Edition packaged by LightSpeed Publishing, Inc.; design by X-Height Studio;
Culinary Americanization: Wes Martin

Library of Congress Cataloging-in-Publication Data Available

2 4 6 8 10 9 7 5 3 1

Published by Hearst Books
Delish is a registered trademark of Hearst Communications, Inc.

www.delish.com

For information about custom editions, special sales, premium and corporate purchases,
please contact Sterling Special Sales Department at 800-805-5489
or specialsales@sterlingpublishing.com.

Distributed in Canada by Sterling Publishing
c/o Canadian Manda Group, 165 Dufferin Street
Toronto, Ontario, Canada M6K 3H6

Manufactured in China

ISBN 978-1-58816-932-7